P1

Harry Smart was born in ‹...›
educated at Batley Gramm‹...›
sity of Aberdeen. His publi‹...›ons include *Criticism and
Public Rationality* (Routledge, 1991). He lives in
Montrose, in the north-east of Scotland, and works as a
freelance journalist and editor. He is married and has one
son.

HARRY SMART

Pierrot

faber and faber

LONDON · BOSTON

First published in 1991
by Faber and Faber Limited
3 Queen Square London WC1N 3AU

Phototypeset by Wilmaset, Birkenhead, Wirral
Printed in England by
Clays Ltd, St Ives plc

Harry Smart is hereby identified as the
author of this work in accordance with Section 77
of the Copyright, Designs and Patents Act 1988.

A CIP record for this book is available from the
British Library.

ISBN 0-571-16279-7

Contents

mind, habituated to apprehend the natures both of all material objects and of things in general

PHILO OF ALEXANDRIA

David and Anna

i.m. Anna Humphries, d. 8 November 1988

Left for the rest of us are simply the free streets,
Imprecise zones where innocence and guilt are
Never quite pinned down as they were in this case.

They wanted more than fingerprints
To put her in the car with him.
They stripped her bed, searching for blood,

Hair, anything she'd left behind when she moved out
From sleep into another schoolday. They proved
Womanhood, showed shattered pieces

Of windscreen to have been kicked out, not broken in
By a stone as he had said. Scientists found slivers
Of black plastic in the glass.

A shoe, the type that she had worn, they discovered
Slices in the sole, glass fragments
Matching glass for glass, the same glass

On a sweater taken from his home.
They matched plastic for plastic. Buttons
From her clothing matched a button from his car, paint

Matched paint. They were linked
By the microscopic and chemical analysis of fragments,
The searching of bedrooms by strangers. They were
   separated

By flowing water, by prolific lies against a closed mouth,
By stone, a silent and a beating heart,
The different states of eyes and of teeth.

Withernsea

i.m. Cicely Harper, 16.11.1908 to 18.11.1988

She whispered, *take this off me*, her gold bracelet,
Earrings, her necklace with the turquoise;
Take this off me, now. Thursday, the day before she died.

Here it is, chain-snake smooth, russet gold and cold blue
Colour of her life's winter,
Warm to the touch.

Power shrivelled, fears grew
As caring people gathered to her side,
I'm very wary of what I take into hospital.

We reinterpret what we questioned months ago,
I don't know where that is now; she didn't.
We learn to value those few things that death has saved.

You take nothing with you, so they say,
But she has taken lying to the grave.
Smoke of bitterness in Humber air;

Cold reflection, lack of proof, her own collusion,
Knowing that her time was short.
We have a few small names, that's all.

Ian and Kay

i.m. Kay Fleming

There was no facing the south
For the sun, it lit the church bravely.

Hymnbook pages turn. Expressions
Flicker from near greeting to the blank

Faces we have practised. We have been here before.
We understand why we are here, why the cars drive slowly,
Just a couple of miles to Sleepyhillock and there's half a mile
Of cars that Kay leads into quiet glory.

The sandy earth's banked steeply, the worn boards only a
    few
Tread, take the weight. The coffin tilts, it's steadied,
    lowered,
Makes a last soft drumbeat as it settles on the hollow bed.
The cords slip silently to the wood.

A stranger's handful knocks in a trinity of gentle
Echoes of ash to ash. Ian's face seems calm. Kay died well,
She spoke of going to be with Jesus when no-one else
    believed
That she was dying, Thursday afternoon, and gone by
    Sunday

Worship. No despair. Nothing to say about pain
From childhood through mothering. She went to the cold
    earth
On a bright day, with the company of tears around her,
The clear song and the curlew for her mourning.

You know me

Well, perhaps not yet,
But you've nothing to worry about –
Look, I'm walking slowly towards you,
Civilized, a gentle gait, almost elegant,
Just a little playfulness, just a trace
Of rhetoric. Stay cool.
Isn't it cold today?
The air's like ice, clean river-grey,
A black-tipped gull wing, calm grey sky;
It's natural to shiver, see
I'm shivering too.
I'll just walk slowly on towards your smile
Saying to myself, *you'll never see the chains*
I carry till you feel the cold grey steel.

Exile

We are not the timeless
Citizens of Parnassus;
We are not at all serene.

No one here is born a poet;
Who would be a poet
Must have a mouth cut,

Must submit to speech,
Must learn the craft by listening
To speech that carries over scars.

A Dream of Wisdom

Hold the still harbours
And prepare the cold, silent harbours
For merriment, of a sort, for dancing,
For the murmuring procession
Of those who must travel.
They must travel far away
To strange hills and plains,
To fields which will not hear their language.

And do not welcome trains.
Do not believe the promises of holiday,
The calling of strangers, the gestures of foreigners
In the morning. Trust only the crack
Of slates, easing themselves against the nails
And the boards, warming slowly after a cold night.

Setup

for Lee Miller

They could have been hard core
Shovelled into heaps, assuming natural
Angles of repose.

Jesus wept!
She's suddenly realized
Identities in tumbled fire-
Clay. At her feet unnatural
Fragments, lacking their living, moist
Pearly gleam.
She knelt and touched a fragment gently
With her fingertips as if soothing a hurt
Child, weeping, cut to the bone.

Survivor

Remembering Al Andalus, the silence of Umayyad Jews
Threading beads in Hebrew's strict diaspora tongue,

There's a man
With a plate in his head.
An iron gourd lines his skull, hidden
Sub-sub-skin, sub-bone. His head

Holds flints, just a handful, and as he shakes
The flints whirl
Through darkness, striking sparks, shooting
Light, memories feed a fiery stream of consciousness.

He has the art, conjuror spinning plates;
The merest tremor of his finger
Keeps a tinnitus of flints on course,
A disciplined holocaust within his crazy mind.

Dante at Birkenau

I will show, as a Christian should,
A good compassion for these fair
Punished ones, whipped in shame.
But I will remember what I have been told,
That they suffer justly;
The inferno is not a place beyond control,
Here, withal, doth Christ's writ run.

I will show, as a Christian should,
Good compassion for these honourable
Men, women and children
Who will not be saved in the last reel, not delivered
Save to the charnel's barbers, their own
Kind who strip them finally, ministering
Rites of passage to bolted iron doors.

I will show such love of God to those
Whom Christendom delivered to the pit
As would hurl judging eyes,
As would hurl judgment's tongue
Among the terrified dying, God
Into Jews' vain crushing of themselves
Against those bolted doors.

Das Haus des Vergessens

In late November we'll gather leaves
Of the year's debatable effort,
Leaves of sycamore, chestnut, elm and birch.
In late November we'll gather leaves

From the ground. Together
We'll pick the finest,
Those least hurt by the wind, intact
Despite the rain and frost.

We'll pick the finest leaves
To dry them by the fire's flame.
We'll dry them to a brittle brown,
Thickly veined, still supple-stalked.

It is a ritual. Each year we do this, taking dried
Leaves in our hands, crumbling skinny
Volumes into the gassy smokeless
Updraught, into the flue's strong pull.

Year 10

What can poetry do against a wall
Of skulls? Lyrical in the Killing Fields,
Should it tread softly? Perhaps
It has no more to do than report
The way that people speak
When they have lost a family, simply,
Father rhymes with mother,
Sister rhymes with brother,

All lost, and still lost. Brother
Rhymes with brother rhymes with
Son and wife and friend and lover
Rhymes with that's enough
Of such simplicities, good neighbour.

Telescope

He's looking away through a black eyepiece,
A Plössl, into the black void; black as black appears
But really filled with light, an infinite number of points
    radiating
Light, most of which doesn't happen to be coming his way.

The stepping motor's silently turning
The mount towards his target. Ada
And her empirical way with celestial ballistics.
She threw the keys down to him. He remembered

Her smile fifteen feet above him. He'd hesitated,
Feared the keys' awkward iron
Angularity unyieldingly beating his hand
If he should catch them, almost

As much as he feared the mental shout
Of his compatriots – imaginary jury.
'Get him a bucket' his father had yelled one afternoon
At Headingley, watching Trueman's benefit. Light in his
    eyes,

The way a thick top edge carries almost to the boundary
But high, and the wind swirls the ball as it falls
So that it's hard to stay under it. He held the keys,
Glad of them falling luckily to his hand.

Those were days of terrestrial observation,
Birds and windows, obscured by heat-shimmer and by
   vibration
From the road. The image shivered into blur
As the light tube quivered.

Florins

Let's keep a place in the digital
Decimal world for an honest word like *florin*.
So much more solid and satisfying
Than *ten pee piece*, so much more
Suggestive of that thickly silver disc,
Hard, yet rubbed to congeniality
With flesh, smooth in the hand.
Florins, a handful of florins,
A man could be happy with a handful of florins.

Tonight I walked home through the town
With three florins tucked comfortably
Between my knuckles, just in case.

The Kingdom and the Wheel

She's a plain woman
And heavy-hipped,
Resilient beneath the whip of everyday
In the plough's grip.

That blue-skinned carter, circumstance,
Can sing his heavy wooden song.
The axle turns within the wheel,
The woman falls, but stands again to carry on.

The brake-rope chafes the socket.
Feet of horses, of women, of every creature
That moves in this cold twilight
Slip in the wet clay.

Plough-tame the landscape
Waits, knowing the years'
Passion, bearing sorrow and its fruit,
Strength, and its fruit is weakness.

As work produces broken lives
The thistle is ploughed under
Yet survives.
The thorn will be crowned king at the last.

The Pierrot

The pierrot's back again, cheerfully
Haunting that moment before sleep
In black and blue and gold.

Today he said to me
Whit wye d'ye aye go on
I'm no awfa happy
Wi the warld the wye it is,
Aye crabbit, aye sair?

So he questions me, wild smiler
Of intimate breath, soft
Trepanning, he makes a gentle invasion
Of the little grey cells,
Intimate as syphilis. It is his way. Suddenly changing roles

He said, See your hands, fair hands,
Not like that man's hands like sea-blocks
Skinned with tigers'
Dull bruises, old tattoos
Of smoky yellow on his claws.

The pierrot's back again tonight
And I have broken the breathing
Of 'eternity', catching breath, carelessly.

Summer Evening

It's time to stand by the window
And be a fine man.
There is, after all, the quiet hour
Before the dances

And the bars begin to be noisy.
The birds' late calling
Louder than the far road's noise
Is broken, often,
By a soft hush, loud whispering;
No-one is alone.
The solitary lie bears repeating.

The time is grey doves.
It's time to stand by the window
Holding an airgun,
Seeking the grey doves in twilight.

Billy Budd

for Paul Durcan

Claggart, that was the name
You chose, and struggled for the reference.
Moby Dick, I think you said, until
I piped up with *Billy Budd*, and
Billy Budd it is, you said, *Everyone*
Should have a Harry in their head
To correct them. Everyone laughed, including me,
Thinking, no doubt, of Ted Hughes
And his mental policeman *à la* Wendy Cope.
I could have added, *I was once in that very play myself*,
As First Lieutenant Ratcliffe – a minor character –
First Lieutenant Smartcliffe as friends used say.
But I didn't speak, merely silently signed
Billy Budd's death warrant, a Claggart job.
I thought, what sort of poems does
A Harry write, in that case? Who polices
His head, who is weary of policing?
Who watches out for the man
Who's ready to close
His Gestapo eyes,
To rest his plodding jackboot feet?
Let the poppies grow on
Your own domestic minefields;
I remember that picture, *The Jewish Bride*,
Indeed, I was once in that very picture myself
Only a decade ago, only last week, only this morning.

Yesterday

Yesterday, pregnant, and with forethought,
She shopped, bought fish, and
Planned to cook this meal.
Today, late in the preparation
We argued, she
Stubborn, sullen-faced and turning
Her back to my questions, my
Anger slammed a door.

I sat alone, she spoke,
Dinner ready,
I walked from the house.
The meal, I presume, is going cold;
My fingers are cold on the pen, and
I am missing Kindertotenlieder on the radio.

There is smoke on the sea-wind, blowing
The soft thump of a calm sea,
The muddy grey-blue rush
Of sand in salt water
Thwashing the breakwater.
There is a dark overcast,
The baked grass stalks in bundles,
Earthbeard.
There is the bright calling of birds from the machair.

Stepping

That's all I went, stepping
From slab to weathered slab,
Waiting
For that dark growl
Low down against the sea's chatter,
Saying,
You're on dangerous ground.

I heard that low-ground growl
Against the summer sun, against
'The white waves' foam, the gentle breeze
That zephyrs o'er the briny foam',
And I moved on, to safety and to you,
My shifting rock, my broken wave,
Hello.

Philosopher at the Beach

Plato: one thing's certain,
He never spent long at the sea-shore
Watching waves. Their rough uniqueness
Would have puzzled him past
Such simplicities as form;
Shadow and reflection and thing-in-itself
Inseparably dynamic, substance and extension
Equally in flux. All waves are
Beyond speech. They will not be
Caught in nets, nor pails, nor pools
Of anyone's devising, not
In nets of filament, not in nets of words
But in wind-sting, in synapses
Free as sea-birds, patient as bone.

Beach

People don't realize that a beach is a dynamic
Zone, that there's a fine balance
Between erosion and deposition. Longshore
Drift tends to keep things on the move, marram,
Sea-thistle, whin, help to pin things down.

Paths worn in the dunes by visitors
Are often the critical factor, a storm
Can scour out a dune-system overnight.
Slowly the small deaths of shell-bearers
Accumulate. Gradually the corners are knocked off

Stones. Constantly the scoop and cast, pestle
Action of the waves wears
Now, here, this into so much dumb shingle,
So many grains of sand, of exoskeletal
Detritus. The perished fragments

Of a tractor tyre, wind-stripped fibres
From a T-shirt, the indigestible portions
Of seaweed holdfasts, egg-cases, feathers
All held in a handful, quite beyond healing.
Always in the grit, the last sharps of quartz.

As countless as the sand on the sea-shore,
And as various as the sea-bones are the bickering
Losses that beaches witness, rarely yielding direct
Evidence of grief, though plenty children weep
Over toys carried out of reach by the wind or the tide.

Here a man lay who'd stood on a stinging creature,
Writhing in pain for an hour, he recovered. There
A young girl lost her virginity; total loss, a bottle
Of valuable liquid lost its stopper. Burly gentlemen
Have always, however, bustled such griefs out of the way

To make room for their own, their philosophical selves.
As Duhig says, 'The reason people like Plato
Never get near beaches is that they're packed with people
Like Demosthenes through Matthew Arnold, MacDiarmid
   to Ted Hughes
Being symbolic about that golfing-torn, that dong-tormented
   sea.'

Incognito

He lived incognito among them
In the Shankhill Road, Jerusalem
And in the guise of a Cathedral
Built entirely of blood-red glass,
Illuminated by choirboys,
Each hanging like a Christmas tree angel
On a golden thread,
Carrying a candle,
Holding out a candle with arms
Of tremendously innocent appearance.

In spite of his chameleon existence
He attracted no small degree of comment
From crowds of benevolent observers
Who gathered each evening
To hear his choirboys
And to see his candles.
Through the blood-red glass
The candles, in the dusk, would spill a light
As of claret, into the streets.

The observers gathered in small groups
To discuss, earnestly, and with care
For the rigour of their argument,
What might be the man's intention,
Dwelling among them in the guise of a Cathedral.

Professors of Logic and Rhetoric
Spontaneously undertook – each evening
Different Professors would visit the phenomenon –
To lead the impromptu discussion groups.
Many of the Professors were men,
Many of the Professors were women,
And they were careful, in the claret candle light,
To give equal opportunities to all
Who wished a part in the debate.

Meanwhile a low humming of assent
Ran, murmured, encouraged.
It was poured out upon them all, a gift of grace
From the walls of the Cathedral.
The choirboys quivered on their golden wires.
They sang high songs of worship
With bright metallic voices
That were almost inaudible. Yet their music,
And the candles, and the humming of the walls
Shed such a spirit upon the debating groups
That each night, each group,
Regardless of the membership and the leadership
Found complete agreement on the fundamental issues.

The Woodcutter's Lot

I've chopped down an awful lot of wood this week,
He said, and he unclenched his teeth.
He unfurled his teeth, he undid the stays
Of his teeth and he said,
I think it's a shame
If a man who's chopped so much wood in a week
Can't have a drink and a painkiller or two.
I prefer Distalgesic, he said, and took another drink
Of his Vin de Pays. *Steady on, dear*, said his wife.
Distalgesic and alcohol, you'll be . . .
Euphoric, he said, I'll be euphoric and
Why not. It'll be a pleasant change, being euphoric.

Self-hypnosis

Now, the thing to remember is this,
You must plan your suggestions carefully;
It's no use just going under
And swimming aimlessly around your unconscious
Wishes and self-castigations.
You must plan your suggestions to the very word,
I am capable of friendship with women, however bizarre
   they may be.

Morning Walks

I walked past the travellers' caravans;
Dogs roused from tea-chests,
From the muddy ground, from among generators

Half covered with sacking or leaning
Wildly in small trailers. Beyond them the broken
Fragments of a mirror, wet in the grass.

I crossed the links' bitter-sweet moss green,
Saw the clean skin of a rabbit, or a dog,
The moist fur and the subcutaneous fat.

Here I sit, perched on the foot of the sea wall,
Waves breaking so close I can see light
Through the cusp. The whiteness of the foam is absolute,

Beyond bone to snow. But the water's force is spent
Just before it reaches me, the waves fold back
To meet the concrete and the iron edge.

Nothing to hear but the crush of water,
Swallow and drench, hollow pattering
As each wave seams into the breakwater.

I can see beneath a blue heaven
Only the blue ocean, steel, white-edged,
And the tawny sand surface that blows bubbles

When the water slides back from it,
Seven herring gulls, beacon white
Beyond the breakers.

II

This is our war, here
On the smooth surface
Darkened by the tide's lick
With only one track man and his dog.

Not a soul to be seen,
Only the rim of dune and hill, breaker
And breakwater, only the blackened stumps
Of the shore nets,

Only the dull sky-white of Scurdie Ness.
No light against the grey sky, darker
To the south. No ships sinking,
Nobody drowning, in fact nothing to laugh at at all,

Here. The only sounds are the cries
Of herring gulls, the endless wave
Song of souls lost at sea. We bury them
In a moment. Walk on.

The tide was high this morning, before dawn
The lower steps were graved in sand
The sea heaved up by the acre,
Wet-packing it dense as flesh.
A woman's tracks, the paw-prints of her dog,
A man dressed in black walks out

From the longshore haze of salt-in-the-mist,
A fat boy appears in a spacy place
Not seeing anyone to see him.
He pours glue into a bag,
Walks in his own way.
He is visited

By a black-headed gull in winter
Plumage that lacks the naming cap.
Bird skips into the steady wind,
Climbs, still-winged by the fat boy's head.
The fat boy watches, gull observes
Him, swings around about this creature

Who stares him silently. The gull rides above
Sand-laden vapour that twists and spins
Flat sheets in the wind low
Against the smooth foreshore, flowing
Around the boy's ankles like a river
Of steam, a pale veil, vanishing.

The idea prevails as if by magic,
Crossing water makes – enchantment –
A man free from the dangers
Of possession or involvement.

We're unlike lights that reach
Over water, over language, barbed
Tongues and trip-wires, searching and reflecting.

Merlin floats stones from Ireland,
Only the mare's tail's left behind.
Over the river and safe away
From thoughts of foreign policy.

V

Oystercatchers mull over the rottweiler's proximity
But disregard the danger, choosing
To pursue food on the field's muddy surfaces.
Approach them if you will,

Those birds will fly
Before you reach them,
Wagging their white isosceles, fast
Into the wet air of the morning.

VI

A skinned Mars Bar, its wrapper still sustains
The illusion of chocolate within.

Feathers, grey and white,
Tacked along each wave's halt.

Seaweed, occasional seashells, carrots
From a bag burst last night, far out to sea.

Dark and flinty stones rest
In wire cages, boxed together, bulging

Heavyweights playing Canute on a giltless throne:
No peacocks, their lower courses steeped in salt.

VII

The old lifeboat house;
Rails and cradle duned in
Sand a man deep.
The doors are closed and there's no way

Out for the boat that isn't there, anyway.
Church-like, built to last
Century's idea, supported by voluntary contributions,
It was a place for the salvation of strangers.

Four lines of footsteps ahead
On the newly uncovered sand. False,
The crust seems firm but my feet sink, and I look at the
    tracks,
Seeing how they too pressed into the soft drift.

I pick my line by the marks the man left
Who had the best path.

VIII

'All that news of thistletop'
Overheard accidentally, more
Than we could bear. It was hard
On both of us, last night's playtime

Woodland crown dismantled,
Brittleness of dried leaves of beech,
Chestnut, elm. The cardboard ring
Survives in a plucked state.

We walk in a brittle fashion
Together to the golden dome. Isobel
Of Spain and her man, uncrowned
The pair of them crush their pillows equally.

That was hard news, too, of what was
Nailed to the walls of Beth Shan.

Gulls overhead and blown
Close enough to follow knowingly.
They slide by smoothly on
A rough wind's buffeting.

Their plumage worn, ragged
At the boundaries, still they fly
The sea's marches, scouring the white foam,
Hunting north and south in the same wind,

Turning and running straight without wingbeats.
Sand furls into the waves' edge,
Foam darkens and subsides
To a slow flat marbled sliding back.

X

Akeldama. May his house become empty;
May no one live in it.
It is written. We remain
In our own house, eternal light

By the river which never breaks its banks,
Ceaseless epiphany, reaching
To the ends of the earth,
The last of the fields of blood.

Sunset

We're experts in the way the sun sets
Across the basin. We know the colours of the sky,
The stages of the tide, evenings' half-mist
Or clarity of air distilled by ice. Therefore we believe

The finest sunsets are those at half-tide under
Skies streaked royal blue and goosefoot pink.
The hills are silhouetted, sand bars
Stand at almost black o' clock, witch-tide,

Between broad bands of estuary water.
The water's calmly incandescent. Light's the light
Of molten glass. Those nights, not more than one in fifty,
We watch the water silently.

We let a great deal stay unspoken,
Considering the landscape, molten glass, river
Light, earth's metal flowing through
Crisp, still night.

On the Edge of Town

The sky never goes beyond
A deep blue, it's a matter of latitude
And of the streetlights' sodium.

At night, though it's not dark, we can see stars
Well above the horizon. Watching, we're alarmed
By flickering wings as if moths drew in

Towards firelight, but our room's as near to darkness
As it can be. They're terns, still flighting in late summer,
Reflecting the glare from the streets.

So we light lamps to blacken the windows
And moths do appear, flapping softly round a head
Of shaken hair, settling on the wallpaper. We brush

The flesh of moths into oblivion,
Bruising the wall with golden paste.
In the morning we wipe the evidence away.

The Night Gulls

We turned by the harbour, light show
Round deep blue belly of water,
Night above deep blue water.
As we turned we saw gulls blown
Across the dark harbour as paper
Caught in arc lights, moment bright –
Moment dark. *I'm surprised to see them*,
Said my mother, *in the darkness*.
To see them so pale against a dark sky.

They reflect the light, I said, *like moons*,
Inevitably. White pages of a diary.
One night a single bird will cut
A perfect arc, an edge of moonlight
On its wings above a silent town;
We shall sit in ruined Bethel,
Arguing.

By Laurencekirk

There must have been great fires today
In hell, and their smoke on the low hills
Blue, cold and bitter, rolling through the valley,
Slow shadows, pouring up, out over the lip of the chasm,
Broad ribbons of mist, smooth, the evening air

Pierced by the vacant eyes of sheep.
Their food, white-balled on the dark earth
Like skulls white-studded on the field,
Thin shadows clouding quietly about.
I like this light, the calm of evening, the restfulness.

Partial Views at Waverley

I cannot say for sure, of course,
And I cannot see clearly
For you are carrying your coat
Over your right arm,
And it is a bulky coat.
But it does seem to me,
From here,
That your left breast
Is a lovely breast.
I would love to hold your left breast in my hand.

Ah, but now she is gone,
Across the empty platform
I can see only the Lady Diana Spencer,
A fine railway engine,
And some scaffolding
Which obscures the dark stone buildings
On the way up to the Mound.

Wake for Doves

In that first morning
The calling of doves was our alarm.
The quietness after the city was like mist,
Moist, the breathing of August leaves,
The lichen green of old orchards,
Dying woodland in an emptied valley,
The whitened green of evening in the paddock.
Stone walls, thick damp plaster,
Faint must larder smell
Of sunlight on the worn stone doorstep,
The warm wooden sill;
Last night's rain drying gently from the garden.

In that first morning we lay quietly together,
Listening, as if we heard
The new light fall upon our bed,
The air falling in the room,
Leaves beyond our window
Tutting the doves' immodest calling;
Drawn from sleep, like silk threads drawn from water.

Naked

I saw a mother and her daughter
Naked as angels, pulling at a man,
The father, for to take him into the sea,
And I loved the daughter in that naked moment
With her teenage around her and
The ripeness of the blue sky.

What came later was envy. Here,
As an azure-sky-on-white-sand
Presence is the envy I feel for that man
To have had, for one moment in his life,
Two beautifully, innocently naked women
Leading him into the sea to play.

Had I ever loved you

Had I ever loved you, gentle
As the summer day's first light
I would have given you the morning air, the white
Hour, silence; let the curtains by the open window rustle,

Hesitate, and move again. I'd have stayed
Beside you, our equal bodies quieted
In tiredness. I'd have singled out
Each contour and each rhythm of you, there to lay

Kisses for your worship. But we are left with bitterness
As fruit of self-deception, yours and mine,
My love. Honesty didn't have a hope in hell
And heaven had no time for faithlessness
Like ours. We gave each other little time
For honesty, and neither loved nor knew each other well.

C. I.

The night was wet, the wind threw tree-shadows
From the lamps in the car park
As arguments against the bedroom walls.
Rain coiled against the windows.

We swam in shadow waters,
In deep hollows of water.
We dreamed of such betrayal as mind can make,
Clerks' treason on summer nights,
Shuddering. Lovemaking supple and unlovely,
The dying of snakes.

A long voice sang,
Hast thou not seen
How thy heart's wishes have been
Granted in what he ordaineth?
And hearts' wishes coiled in the room
Wherein we swam, wherein we were at sea.

Birdsong

The cry passed through the window and into the street,
It came no louder than the sound of birdsong on a rainy
   night.
Hours later, rain treading the slates,
The sound of women climbing a wooden staircase,
Birds were sleeping,
There was no song, but the gentle rainfall.

In the morning was brightness
Shining over wet gravestones,
A quiet day of sunshine after rain.
The calling of sparrows was keen as a sharp knife on glass.

The Queen of the Field of Early Summer

She spread her white skirt neatly,
Her broad white linen skirt upon the grass.
She smoothed the linen clean against the ground. There

Some will serve her wearing polished helmets,
Some have left the winter's dust alone.
Some have made their hair lie tidy

With an ivory comb
And some are still untidy as they rose.
Some have mended thoughts at dawn

While others have not troubled
Their souls, or God, with penitence.
But all their boots

And all their horses' hooves
Will stamp the same earth down
Through linen white as silver

Where her skirt is spread upon the ground.
The earth will take a true impression
As they quit themselves like men upon the ground.

For the sowing time is over
And there's nothing left to do
But to watch the harvest ripen

Through the green and gold of summer
To whitened heads that wait the reaper.
Where she spread her skirt upon the ground

She will gather in the autumn,
Such a gathering of whiteness
From the ground, from the ground, from the ground.

Gwên Ystrad

Gwên Ystrad left many a man-
Thing lying unwanted in grass

Or in the places where mud was pounded
Up from the roots to seize

Stem and flowering head, stolon
And rhizome laid bare and severed

To dry in the cold wind. He
Walked gently on the beaten ground.

He did not break the bruised reed,
He let the cold wind blow

His smouldering rush to a flame
For the tall fire that he built.

Madagascar

Madagascar is where I was born,
A terrible land, if I remember my childhood accurately,
And where I grew up in a household filled with
Strange drawings of even stranger practices,
Some of which were sexual, and others
Barely conceivable as human.

I remember a day in the summer of my thirteenth year.
The tension in the catapult was terrible,
Strong the catch that gripped the bowl
That held the burning stone.
Thwack. The missile flew
To circumnavigate a fiery nobleman.

How sadly she weeps, the woman who walks
Alone in the meadows
And the saddle empty.
She walks through these same meadows
Each evening from summer to late autumn,
Alone, in a land I'd rather call Madagascar.

1945

i.m. D.B.

In the sunlight, from a tree
In the far corner of the square
Hang pears, fat and heavy,
Thick-skinned and simply hanging, silent
As theologians.

The officer with the damaged arm
Orders two of his men
To flog a young woman,
Which duty they perform efficiently,
Placing her across a trestle in the middle of the square

In the sunlight. The square is hot,
White dust and bright light fill the air, quietness
Broken only by the cries of the woman
And the heavy thwack of the whips on her back.
It is too warm, really, to be out of doors

But the theologians are beyond caring.
Their blind eyes are gathering dust.
There is no breeze to comfort them,
They are blind as pears,
Fat, and heavy, and simply hanging.

A Bowl of Jewels

They were men of glass, hard,
Not fragile, not brittle and unyielding
But molten, liquid and supple.
Their blood was hotter than the melting of rock.
They glowed. Their minds were furnaces.

They came down to the riverside.
There they quenched their thirst,
And there they took sweetmeats,
A bowl of jewels. A broad bowl of crystalled light,
Diamonds and sapphires, and the light light dust
Across them like the sugar on a fondant.
Rubies, sweet, and castered emeralds were there.

And as they ate, the jewels melted in their mouths.
And as they ate, each form took up the colour of the gem.
There sat a man of molten glass, taking the succulent colour
Of a ruby deep within him, there another shone sapphire.
The hot air shimmered around them.
Calmly they talked of cataclysm, of the burning core
Loosed upon the surface, of the days when they walked
Barefoot across the smoking lava fields. The brimstone tore
The air, the sulphur was their condiment.

When they rose from their rich feast it was night-time,
Their bodies burned the darkness as they walked.
They were refreshed, and they had zeal for judgment.
They had men to meet, and questions to ask them.
They bore light through the darkness
For the followers of Lucifer.
They bore justice through the night
For the men who dwelt on the cold islands.
They bore weapons keener and more terrible
Than any sword to judge the hearts of men.

Aysgarth

Rain scattering; the hillside rises from the river.
When the men and women are gone
From the graveside
This will remain,
A sparrow flying into the wind,
A trail of birdsong blown down the valley
And lost over the sound of water.

'Exile'
See 'Intimate Parnassus' by Patrick Kavanagh.

'Das Haus des Vergessens'
'The house of forgetting'; the phrase is taken from 'Der Sand aus den Urnen' by Paul Celan.

'Beach'
'though plenty children weep' – to drop the 'of' after 'plenty' is a Scots idiom.
'As Duhig says . . .' – the comment is by Ian Duhig, in response to 'Philosopher at the Beach'.

'Morning Walks'
VIII – 'Beth Shan'; see 1 Samuel 31:1–10.
X – 'Akeldama'; see Acts 1:18–19.

'Gwên Ystrad'
The valley of Gwen, now known as Wensleydale. It was the scene of one of the great victories of Urien of Rheged, as described by Taliesin in Gwaith Gwênystrad (The Battle of Wensleydale). See the translation of Meirion Pennan (*Taliesin: Poems*, Llanerch, 1988).

Poems from this collection previously appeared in the following magazines, whose editors I would like to thank: *Agenda, Oxford Poetry, Lines Review, Outposts, West Coast Magazine, Poetry and Audience*. 'A Bowl of Jewels' appeared in the Prizewinners' Anthology of the 1987 National Poetry Competition, and 'Morning Walks' was shortlisted for the 1990 Arvon International Poetry Competition.